Phonics and Word Study

 Continental Press

ISBN 978-0-8454-3853-4

Table of Contents

Read each definition. Then write the missing consonant to complete the word. Use the letters **b, f, h, j, k, l, m, n, p, r, t, v, w,** and **y.**

1. a cold season _____inter

2. a long trip _____ourney

3. a pot for boiling water _____ettle

4. the time after now _____uture

5. empty _____acant

6. the head of a city government _____ayor

---

7. meat often eaten for breakfast baco_____

8. a drink made from the juice of apples cide_____

9. a pail bucke_____

10. a list of events progra_____

11. twelve of something doze_____

12. the fast run of a horse gallo_____

---

13. to disappear va_____ish

14. a person who makes bread, cakes, and pies ba_____er

15. a mixture of green vegetables sa_____ad

16. a deep valley with steep sides can_____on

17. the taste of something fla_____or

18. a covering to protect the head hel_____et

In the following group, the last letter in each word is the same as the first letter in the next word.

1. a person who flies an airplane _____i_____o_____

2. a spring flower _____u_____i_____

3. a student _____u_____i_____

4. a sour, juicy fruit _____e_____o_____

5. not at any time _____e_____e_____

Some consonants have more than one sound.

c /k/ as in *cut*
/s/ as in *city*
(with i) /sh/ as in *special*

g /g/ as in *geese*
/j/ as in *giant*

s /s/ as in *salt*
/z/ as in *rose*
(with u) /sh/ as in *sure*
(with u) /zh/ as in *treasure*

t /t/ as in *tag*
(with u) /ch/ as in *fortune*
(with i) /ch/ as in *question*
(with i) /sh/ as in *station*

Above each boldface letter or letter combination, write the symbol that stands for its sound.

1. hu**g**e

2. your**s**elf

3. de**s**erve

4. vine**g**ar

5. u**s**ual

6. ability

7. fu**t**ure

8. **c**hocolate

9. oran**g**e

10. mu**s**eum

11. i**c**y

12. offi**ci**al

13. de**s**ign

14. plea**s**ure

15. ra**g**e

16. chee**s**e

17. oxy**g**en

18. bar**g**ain

19. **t**umble

20. hin**g**e

21. re**g**ular

22. rid**g**e

23. mea**s**ure

24. an**c**ient

25. **s**u**g**ar

26. introdu**c**e

27. pa**ti**ent

28. pre**ci**ous

29. si**t**ua**ti**on

30. mu**si**cian

31. in**c**rease

32. a**c**tion

33. va**c**a**ti**on

34. vi**ci**ous

35. fau**c**et

36. re**sc**ue

37. **c**rea**t**ure

38. **c**arria**g**e

39. an**c**estor

40. **g**es**t**ure

In some words, two or three consonants are together and their sounds are blended. They are called consonant blends. These are the most common blends.

br cr dr fr gr pr tr
bl cl fl gl pl st
sp sc sk sw sm sn
scr spl spr str squ tw

Complete each word below by adding one of the blends above to the letters shown.

____ ____ift   ____ ____een   ____ ____oke   ____ ____ept

____ ____ift   ____ ____ ____een   ____ ____ ____oke   ____ ____ept

____ ____ing   ____ ____ame   ____ ____ell   ____ ____in

____ ____ing   ____ ____ame   ____ ____ell   ____ ____in

____ ____ing   ____ ____ame   ____ ____ell   ____ ____in

Read each definition. Then write the missing consonant blend to complete each word.

1. the cost of something   ____ ____ice

2. to sparkle   ____ ____inkle

3. to press together   ____ ____ ____eeze

4. a nail on the toe of an animal   ____ ____aw

5. to break into pieces   ____ ____ ____it

6. a squeaking sound   ____ ____eak

7. to growl sharply   ____ ____arl

8. to welcome   ____ ____eet

9. something used for weighing   ____ ____ale

10. to take long steps when walking   ____ ____ ____ide

11. to hang down   ____ ____oop

12. a person who travels to get new information   ex____ ____orer

13. ran away   ____ ____ed

14. to use words to tell about something   de ____ ____ ____ibe

15. to move smoothly   ____ ____ide

Two consonant letters together that make one sound are called a consonant digraph. These are the most common digraphs.

ch	ck	ng
sh	th	wh

Complete each word by adding one of the digraphs above to the letters shown.

____ ____ick   ____ ____ere   ____ ____ief   ____ ____en

____ ____ick   ____ ____ere   ____ ____ief   ____ ____en

pa____ ____   sti____ ____   tra____ ____   wi____ ____

pa____ ____   sti____ ____   tra____ ____   wi____ ____

Read each definition. Circle the word in each pair that fits the definition.

1. to have a desire for		wing	wish
2. a male ruler		kick	king
3. to cut into small pieces		chop	shop
4. a footprint		trash	track
5. a low, crying sound		whine	shine
6. a kind of tree		birth	birch
7. a bag		sack	sash
8. the wound from a bee		stick	sting
9. picked out		chose	those
10. to make quiet		hush	hung
11. a male deer		buck	bush
12. to excite		shrill	thrill
13. to hold on to		cling	click
14. the grain used to make flour		cheat	wheat
15. to talk in a quick way		shatter	chatter

Consonant blends and consonant digraphs may be at the beginning of a word, in the middle, or at the end.

In the paragraph below, circle the words with consonant blends and underline those with consonant digraphs. (Do not underline the word *the*.)

Last winter our family had all the popcorn we could eat. The summer before that, we raised our own vegetables. Our backyard in the city is tiny. So Mom and Dad paid to use a garden plot in the county park. Often we stayed to work on it until dusk. We each used a shovel and some other tools. Many nights we took a picnic dinner along with us. In May, little sprouts could be seen. Only the radishes were ready. But by July, we had a garden full of beautiful vegetables. My favorites were the watermelons, the best I've ever tasted. I liked the popcorn, too. Winter nights didn't seem complete unless we ate some. When we discuss if we'd like a garden again, we all agree. Yes!

Write the words from the paragraph that contain consonant blends and consonant digraphs in the correct column. Show the position of the blend or digraph by writing the word in the correct row.

	Consonant Blends	Consonant Digraphs
Beginning	_____ _____ _____	_____ _____ _____
Middle	_____ _____ _____	_____ _____ _____
End	_____ _____ _____	_____ _____ _____

The consonant digraph **ch** has three sounds.

/ch/ **ch**oice   /k/ e**ch**o   /sh/ musta**ch**e

The consonant digraph **th** has two sounds.

/th/ **th**ick   /<u>th</u>/ <u>th</u>is

On the line in front of each word, write the symbol that stands for the sound of the boldface letters.

_____ 1. au**th**or

_____ 2. monar**ch**

_____ 3. ba**th**e

_____ 4. para**ch**ute

_____ 5. sou**th**

_____ 6. pin**ch**

_____ 7. weal**th**

_____ 8. **th**us

_____ 9. **ch**aracter

_____ 10. **ch**urn

_____ 11. whe**th**er

_____ 12. **th**irsty

_____ 13. **th**ose

_____ 14. an**ch**or

_____ 15. bo**th**er

_____ 16. **ch**ill

_____ 17. ma**ch**ine

_____ 18. ex**ch**ange

_____ 19. mou**th**ful

_____ 20. a**ch**e

_____ 21. en**ch**ant

The sound of /sh/ can be spelled five ways.

| s **sure** | sh **sh**y | ch ma**ch**ine | ci spe**ci**al | ti men**ti**on |

On the line in front of each word, write the letter or letters that stand for the sound of /sh/ in the word.

_____ 1. precious

_____ 2. ashore

_____ 3. cautious

_____ 4. fashion

_____ 5. motion

_____ 6. ancient

_____ 7. mustache

_____ 8. astonish

_____ 9. sugar

_____ 10. patience

_____ 11. shelter

_____ 12. delicious

_____ 13. parachute

_____ 14. attention

_____ 15. official

_____ 16. relation

_____ 17. vanish

_____ 18. musician

_____ 19. station

_____ 20. situation

_____ 21. shawl

Each vowel has a short vowel sound. Say the following words. Listen for the short vowel sound.

/a/	/e/	/i/	/o/	/u/
cap	jet	tin	hot	rug

In the paragraph below, circle each word with a short vowel sound.

I like to fish. All that I need is a rod, a line, fresh bait, plus a weight to hold the bait down. The rest is easy. First I gather the worms. I find a quiet place at a nearby pond for my fun. I drop the line before I prop the rod by a rock. At times I lie on the grassy bank to wait for a nibble on the line. Each season I check around for a new spot. But I also keep a few special places to myself. My uncle can't seem to figure me out. He didn't know girls liked such things. I can't explain, either. I just like to fish.

Write each circled word next to the letter that stands for its short vowel sound. If the same word is circled more than once, write it only one time.

a _____ _____ _____

e _____ _____ _____

i _____ _____ _____

o _____ _____ _____

u _____ _____ _____

The sound of long **a** /ā/ has six spelling patterns.

ea—gr**ea**t   ai—p**ai**d   ey—th**ey**   ay—h**ay**   ei—**ei**ght

Another spelling pattern is aCe.

   a/consonant/silent e—c**ave**, g**ate**

In the paragraphs below, circle the words with the long **a** sound.

   For my birthday, my parents gave me a stamp album. I check all our mail now. Our neighbors save stamps for me, too. You can also buy stamps from faraway countries at a hobby shop. I have to pay for them myself. I trade stamps with other collectors, too.

   My friends collect all kinds of things. Maya collects rocks. Some are plain, but others are quite beautiful. Eduardo collects butterflies in a case. He is careful not to break their wings when he mounts them. Rochelle has been collecting coins for eight months. Her collection already contains an unusual 1914 penny. Dave has a great collection of baseball cards. And his dad collects old toy trains and planes.

On the line in front of each definition, write the correct circled word from the paragraphs above.

_____   1. people who live near one another

_____   2. connected lines of cars pulled along a track

_____   3. to put aside for the future

_____   4. common or ordinary

_____   5. machines that have wings and fly

_____   6. includes

_____   7. to exchange one thing for another

_____   8. a container to put things in

_____   9. distant

_____   10. a game played with a ball and bat

The sound of long **e** /ē/ has seven spelling patterns.

e—w**e**	ea—l**ea**p	ei—c**ei**ling	y—bus**y**
ee—w**ee**k	ie—ch**ie**f		ey—donk**ey**

In the paragraph below, circle the words with the long **e** sound.

Think of a very large object that is shaped like a giant cigar and travels in the sky. It can carry as many as fifty passengers. It is a blimp. This airship is lifted into the air by a special gas that is lighter than air. Some of the old blimps were up to eight hundred feet long. They could reach a speed of seventy miles an hour. Blimps were once a popular means of travel. Then travelers received news of several bad accidents, and the passenger service ended. Today, some experts believe that blimps should be tried again. They think blimps can be flown safely now. Other key reasons are also important. Blimps run quietly. They need only a small landing field. And they cost less money to run than airplanes.

On the line in front of each definition, write the correct circled word from the paragraph above.

_____ **1.** to think of as true

_____ **2.** a cleared area of land

_____ **3.** important, main

_____ **4.** half of one hundred

_____ **5.** causes of something

_____ **6.** without accident or harm

_____ **7.** something used to pay costs

_____ **8.** a measure of length

_____ **9.** a measure of movement

_____ **10.** got

The sound of long **i** /ī/ has four spelling patterns.

ie—t**ie**   igh—t**igh**t   y—sp**y**

Another spelling pattern is i**Ce**.

i/consonant/silent e—m**ine**, b**ike**

In the paragraph below, circle the words with the long **i** sound.

Some types of popular beliefs have to do with luck. There are people who believe that you shouldn't walk under a ladder or open an umbrella inside a house. One of the most famous of these beliefs has to do with the number thirteen. Many people thought about it during our third moon flight. The spaceship was called Apollo 13. The ride into space began quite well on a bright Saturday in April of 1970. The captain was Jim Lovell. Everything was fine for two days. Then came word of an accident on the ship 206,000 miles from Earth. It happened on April 13. People were frightened for Lovell and his crew. Everyone feared that they might die. The world was delighted when they arrived home safely at last. It would be a lie, though, to say that the accident didn't cause people to think again about the number thirteen.

On the line in front of each definition, write the correct circled word from the paragraph above.

_____   1. afraid

_____   2. an untrue statement

_____   3. pleased and happy

_____   4. to stop living

_____   5. could

_____   6. reached a place

_____   7. a trip in which a person is carried on something

_____   8. a trip through the air

_____   9. certain kinds

The sound of long **o** /ō/ has five spelling patterns.

   o—n**o**   oa—fl**oa**t   ow—bl**ow**   ough—th**ough**

Another spelling pattern is o**C**e.

   o/consonant/silent e—h**ope**, dr**ove**

In the paragraph below, circle the words with the long **o** sound.

Do you usually have a snack when you get home? Many people go straight to the refrigerator. They look for something cold to drink. Or they reach for a special treat. They look for sweets, like candy or doughnuts. These snack foods are loaded with sugar, though. They may taste good, but they aren't good for your body. Too much sugar can ruin your teeth and cause weight problems. It's easy to learn to choose snacks that aren't so bad for you. Try drinks that are low in sugar. Or make a float with milk and fruit. Eat fresh fruit or roasted peanuts. You can also mix fresh fruit slices with the nuts for a tasty treat. Whenever you eat good snack foods, you'll know you have done your body a favor.

On the line in front of each definition, write the correct circled word from the paragraph above.

_____   1. too

_____   2. to understand

_____   3. not high

_____   4. a sweet drink containing fruit or ice cream

_____   5. filled

_____   6. the place where you live

_____   7. cooked in an oven

_____   8. small treats shaped like a ring

_____   9. even so

_____   10. the opposite of "stop"

These vowel sounds also have more than one spelling pattern.

ū—mule, few   ü—zoo, through, new, suit, blue

The letters oo also have the sound of /u̇/ in book.

In each group of words below, circle the two words with the same vowel sound.

1. cube	rude	view	11. zoo	flew	found
2. hook	brook	troop	12. wood	bruise	grew
3. blue	trout	group	13. drew	chew	shook
4. look	school	crew	14. through	mule	noon
5. few	cute	true	15. doubt	mood	scoop
6. mouse	smooth	flute	16. fruit	guide	blew
7. juice	quit	tooth	17. good	clue	loose
8. cook	goose	pool	18. shoot	too	loud
9. stood	threw	soup	19. shout	gloom	choose
10. took	soon	good	20. pew	scout	huge

In each sentence below, circle the two words with the same vowel sound. Use only those vowel spellings listed at the top of the page.

1. A cool fruit salad is perfect on a hot summer day.

2. Only a few of those huge logs will be cut and shaped into chairs.

3. Water the blue flowers, and they will not droop.

4. I placed worms on the hook and then dropped the line into the brook.

5. We viewed a film about the use of soybeans.

6. The detectives searched the crew for clues that could help solve the mystery.

7. After the storm, a group of children threw snowballs at each other.

8. The astronauts made a loop around the moon and then came home.

A single vowel followed by **r** is not long or short. The **r** changes the sound of the vowel. When **or** follows **w,** it has the sound in w**or**k and w**or**d.

ar	er	ir	or	ur
p**ar**t	s**er**ve	d**ir**t	f**or**k	c**ur**l

Complete each sentence with one of the words below the blank.

1. Angie _____ her elbow when she fell off her skateboard.
   hurt, hut

2. One of the most frightening sea animals is the _____.
   shack, shark

3. Jodie's long _____ got caught in the elevator door.
   skirt, skit

4. Sean tied the package carefully with heavy _____.
   cod, cord

5. By crawling through the earth, a _____ helps the soil to breathe.
   wore, worm

6. Cover your mouth when you sneeze, or you'll spread _____.
   gems, germs

The spelling **ear** has three sounds.

1. n**ear**   2. b**ear**   3. **ear**n

Complete each sentence with one of the words below the blank. Then write the number of the key word above that has the same sound.

1. Did you _____ the sirens last night? ____
   heal, hear

2. I would like to _____ to speak Spanish. ____
   lean, learn

3. Toni likes to _____ sandals in the summer. ____
   wear, weak

4. Ripe, sweet _____ are my favorite fruit. ____
   peaks, pears

When **i** is followed by **ld, nd,** or **gh,** it usually has the long vowel sound.

night

When **o** is followed by **ld, lt,** or **st,** it usually has the long vowel sound.

ghost

In the paragraph below, circle all the words with a long **i** or long **o** sound.

Last weekend, Rita gave a costume party. Some people looked frightful. However, a gentle ghost with a mild manner didn't shock anyone. Other people dressed funny. A wild colt had canes for front legs. Jerome came as a gold bird. With his loose feathers, he looked ready to molt. Jack Frost was there, too. He actually made me feel cold. After everyone saw everyone else, we guessed who was behind each mask. Lee got a new CD for getting the most right. Then we had a treasure hunt for nuts and apples. We could keep whatever we could find. All in all, it was a great party.

On the line in front of each definition, write the correct circled word from the paragraph above.

_____ 1. the opposite of lose

_____ 2. a young horse

_____ 3. very scary

_____ 4. more than the others

_____ 5. the opposite of tame

_____ 6. extremely chilly

_____ 7. a valuable metal

_____ 8. correct

_____ 9. in back of

_____ 10. soft, not strong

Sounds of **ild, ind, igh, old, olt,** and **ost**   17

The letter **y** can represent a vowel sound or a consonant sound. When it stands for a vowel sound, it has the sound of long **i** or long **e**.

Consonant **y**—yes (y)   Vowel **y**—fry /ī/ or city /ē/

In the paragraph below, circle the words in which **y** is a consonant, and underline those in which it is a vowel.

I've never seen more than a few sparrows in our yard. Even so, I decided to build a birdfeeder. After I hung it on a tree branch, I waited nearby to see if some birds would come along. The sparrows came first. Before long, a noisy mockingbird appeared. It chased off the other birds. It also chased our puppy, which ran off with an unhappy yelp. Later, a beautiful redbird decided to fly over and try the feeder. As he ate, he sang a pretty song. His mate sang a reply. Next a bright yellow bird stopped by. It looked like a canary. It seemed young and shy. Mom said it was a goldfinch. I keep the feeder filled with plenty of seed. All year long, I'll be able to watch the birds that come to our backyard.

Write each circled and underlined word in the correct column.

y — Consonant	y — long i	y — long e
_____	_____	_____
_____	_____	_____
_____	_____	_____
_____	_____	_____
_____	_____	_____

The vowel spelling **ea** has more than one sound.

/ē/	/ā/	/e/
seal	steak	thread

In the paragraph below, circle each word with the vowel spelling **ea**.

Every living creature is special in one way or another. Ostriches are great runners, and penguins are good swimmers. Both birds have feathers, but neither can fly. Giant pandas are quite large, and yet they are like raccoons in some ways. Both animals have strong claws and very sharp teeth. But pandas eat plants instead of meat. Then there are anteaters, which love to feast on an anthill. Beavers have tails that look like paddles. They work hard while otters seem to live just to have fun. They get their pleasure sliding down a mud bank into a lake. Bats are dreadful looking animals. Although many of them can't see very well, they always know where they're heading. Finally, there are the whales. These animals live underwater. Every once in a while, they take a break to come up for a breath of air. Even the whales know that they aren't fish.

Write each circled word in the correct column.

/ē/	/ā/	/e/
_____	_____	_____
_____	_____	_____
_____		_____
_____		_____
_____		_____
_____		_____

Each of these sounds has two different spellings.

/ou/	/ō/	/oi/
loud	though	joy
town	bowl	join

In the paragraph below, circle those words with the **ow** spelling, underline those with the **ou** spelling, and box those with the **oi** or **oy** spelling.

Today more and more people are talking about solar power. Even many boys and girls have used it. When we burn a hole in paper with a magnifying glass, we are using solar energy. That's using it as a toy, though. Scientists are interested in knowing more. They want to use the sun's energy to cook food and boil water. They'd like to heat houses with it. They want to warm buildings when clouds fill the sky, snow covers the ground, and the north wind blows. Other kinds of fuel, like oil and coal, are running low. So scientists see the sun as the best fuel choice for the future. The next time the sun shines in a nearby window, think solar.

Write each circled, underlined, and boxed word in the correct column.

/ou/	/ō/	/oi/
_____	_____	_____
_____	_____	_____
_____	_____	_____
_____	_____	_____
_____	_____	_____
_____	_____	_____

The vowel sound you hear in **talk** /ô/ has several spellings.

/ô/	/ô/	/ô/	/ô/	/ô/
walk	toss	fault	draw	brought

In each group of words below, circle the two words with the same vowel sound. Underline the letters that stand for the sound /ô/. Use only the vowel spellings above.

1. yawn	wall	young		11. round	haunt	walk
2. through	off	taught		12. dawn	fault	rolled
3. caught	soup	fought		13. tall	bat	hawk
4. call	sought	mop		14. coffee	lawn	rock
5. loud	dog	paw		15. show	cross	shawl
6. cause	cloth	should		16. talk	claw	rough
7. frost	most	small		17. group	ought	jaw
8. knot	bald	law		18. squawk	ton	born
9. fall	tough	haul		19. glad	all	crawl
10. hall	stop	pause		20. raw	cost	ghost

In each sentence below, circle the two words with the sound /ô/. Use the vowel spellings listed at the top of the page.

1. I get up at dawn and walk a mile.

2. I saw the ball roll into the bushes, but now I can't find it.

3. Pedro brought salt to the picnic, but not pepper.

4. Allen thought the accident was his fault.

5. Cindy bought her sister a shawl as a gift.

6. The group paused as they entered the haunted funhouse.

7. You ought to be cautious when you drive.

8. I hauled at least six boxes of bricks over the lawn to build a new fireplace.

9. Hawks and bald eagles are members of the same bird family.

The vowel spelling ou has more than one sound.

/ō/	/ô/	/ü/	/u/	/ou/
d**ou**gh	br**ou**ght	y**ou**	t**ou**ch	h**ou**se

In the paragraph below, circle each word with the vowel spelling **ou**.

    Last Saturday my cousin and I went to a public sale in the country. It was held outside, so we brought lawn chairs with us. We were the youngest people there. Sometimes it can be tough for youths in a group so large. But we soon understood what all the loud shouting meant. Although there were thousands of things to buy, we bought only a few. After a while, we walked through the crowd to find some food. We each had chicken soup and a doughnut. We never thought we'd stay long. But it was such fun that we decided we ought to stay the whole day.

Write each circled word next to the symbol that stands for the sound of **ou** in the word.

/ō/   _____

             _____

/ô/   _____   _____

             _____   _____

/ü/   _____   _____

             _____   _____

/u/   _____   _____

             _____   _____

/ou/   _____   _____

             _____   _____

The letters **qu** represent the sound /kw/.

quilt

The letters **gu** represent the sound /g/.

guest

The letters **gh** and **ph** can represent the sound /f/.

rough

elephant

In the paragraph below, circle each word with one of these letter combinations.

Guess what Dad brought home last month—CB radio equipment! We all read the guide to begin with. Soon we were ready to send and receive messages. At first the radio was quiet. Then it started to squeak and squeal. It even made a sound like a cough. We fixed the noises quickly enough. We all had to laugh when we heard other people's "handles." One person is called Daffy Dolphin. Another is King's Guard. Dad gave us the handle "Tongue Twister." This radio is like having guests in the house all the time. It's even better than a cell phone because you get to meet new people.

Write each circled word in the correct column.

/kw/	/g/	/f/
_____	_____	_____
_____	_____	_____
_____	_____	_____
_____	_____	_____
_____	_____	_____

The ending **-ed** has three sounds. When it is added to some words, it forms a separate syllable.

/əd/ lift**ed**   /d/ cheer**ed**   /t/ rush**ed**

In the paragraph below, circle the words in which the ending **-ed** has been added.

Many doctors and scientists have discovered ways to save lives. One person who stands out is Charles Drew. Charles grew up in a poor section of Washington, D.C. He enjoyed sports and learned quickly. In high school, Drew played in four different sports and still succeeded in getting good grades. He then attended college and medical school, where he earned high marks. After Drew finished medical school, he returned to Washington to teach. Later, while working in a hospital, Dr. Drew expressed an interest in studying blood. He worked and developed a way to store blood until it was needed. This had never been done before. It was important because World War II had just started. People wounded in battle needed blood. Drew's discovery has helped millions of other people, too. Sadly, his own life ended early. His car crashed one night in 1950. We can be thankful Charles Drew gave so much while he was alive.

Write each circled word in the correct column. Divide into syllables the words in which **-ed** adds a syllable.

/əd/	/d/	/t/
_____	_____	_____
_____	_____	_____
_____	_____	_____
_____	_____	_____
_____	_____	_____
_____	_____	_____

When you are reading, words can look alike. Read carefully. Each word should make sense.

mean   main   palace   place

Complete each sentence with one of the words below the blank.

1. The highway followed the path of an American Indian _____.
   trial, trail

2. Steam rose from the bowl of hot _____.
   soup, soap

3. We waited on the sidewalk for the light to _____.
   chance, change

4. The _____ gas station is about eleven miles away.
   closet, closest

5. An _____ in his side forced Leroy out of the race.
   arch, ache

6. The car _____ on the ice and spun completely around.
   skipped, skidded

7. In which _____ were your grandparents born?
   nation, nature

8. After each baseball game, Hiko _____ about his hits.
   beasts, boasts

9. Please _____ me to return my library books today.
   remain, remind

10. The new band uniforms have a white _____ down each pant leg.
    stripe, stride

11. During the _____, Sandy played a solo on the trumpet.
    concern, concert

12. At the bottom of this steep hill, the road _____ sharply to the right.
    curves, carves

When you are reading, words can look alike. Read carefully. Each word should make sense.

Complete each sentence with one of the words below the blank.

1. Seat belts are an important safety _____.
   future, feature

2. There is _____ we can do to fix the bike.
   noting, nothing

3. Simon pulled a _____ when he lifted the heavy box.
   muscle, musical

4. I _____ what time it is?
   wonder, wander

5. Please leave your wet _____ on the porch.
   boats, boots

6. The black car _____ down the dark street.
   vanished, varnished

7. We must hurry so that _____ be on time.
   well, we'll

8. A narrow _____ leads to the river.
   path, patch

9. There are seven _____ in the play.
   charters, characters

10. Are you _____ of the new bus schedule?
    awake, aware

11. The _____ called a strike.
    empire, umpire

12. The team left the _____ after the game.
    field, filed

In each row, circle the words that contain the sound shown at the beginning of the row.

1. /k/   carve   echo   cement   arch   cub

2. /s/   base   chose   sugar   cider   solid

3. /sh/   coach   official   motion   lash   sure

4. /z/   wisdom   muscle   custom   design   observe

5. /zh/   usual   pleasure   desire   result   television

6. /g/   gesture   freight   fog   gym   gulp

7. /j/   ledge   original   regular   gently   urge

8. /t/   captain   within   actor   protest   latch

9. /ch/   mustache   pinch   future   anchor   chirp

10. /th/   health   thee   truth   author   thirsty

11. /th/   bathe   booth   thus   smooth   warmth

12. /y/   cycle   canyon   navy   style   yelp

13. /f/   dolphin   height   paragraph   tough   dough

14. /kw/   tongue   question   quit   equal   guide

15. /t/   touched   ruined   grounded   gripped   shocked

16. /d/   limped   blamed   sealed   mapped   carved

17. /əd/   posted   peeled   aided   shifted   vanished

In each row, circle the words that contain the same vowel sound.

1. death   guest   breathe   bet   scent   rein

2. known   prop   lodge   cord   rod   through

3. bunch   churn   snug   tough   rude   blood

4. bait   hey   leash   clank   tray   weigh

5. pearl   speed   heap   wealth   chief   seize

6. file   veil   guide   height   grind   sink

7. cost   boast   frown   shown   post   stole

8. view   cube   mud   growl   curve   huge

9. bloom   youth   bruise   dough   clue   flood

10. chart   stare   ward   barge   shark   arch

11. glare   worth   blurt   fern   twirl   wore

12. swarm   scarce   pear   starve   flare   prayer

13. smear   rare   mere   stern   oar   fear

14. port   torch   work   sore   score   court

15. ought   mount   rough   owe   trout   scowl

16. boil   joy   choice   sly   doubt   tow

17. salt   boss   haul   hound   grown   frog

A contraction is made from two or more words written together. An apostrophe (') represents the letter or letters that have been left out.

Write the contraction for each of these word pairs.

1. I will _____
2. you are _____
3. should not _____
4. here is _____
5. he had _____
6. we are _____

7. he will _____
8. has not _____
9. we have _____
10. she has _____
11. you had _____
12. you would _____

Write the words that were used to form each of these contractions.

1. I'm _____
2. you'll _____
3. don't _____
4. you've _____
5. aren't _____
6. we'd _____

7. he's _____
8. we'll _____
9. there's _____
10. hadn't _____
11. she'd _____
12. I'll _____

Complete each sentence with one of the words below the line.

1. _____ the hammer Dad needed this morning.
    Here's, Hears

2. The front _____ on my bike is bent.
              wheel, we'll

3. When _____sick, try to get some extra sleep.
         your, you're

4. _____ no glue left to finish my art project.
    Theirs, There's

5. Trent will win the race if _____ just keep running.
                              he'll, heel

6. If we want to be on time, _____ better leave now.
                             weed, we'd

A compound word is formed by joining two or more small words.

Draw a line to connect two words that form a compound word. Write the words on the lines.

gold	shield	1. _____
wind	port	2. _____
air	house	3. _____
drug	quarters	4. _____
some	fish	5. _____
light	shore	6. _____
head	road	7. _____
sea	store	8. _____
rail	how	9. _____

Sometimes a compound word is written as one word, sometimes as separate words, and sometimes with a hyphen connecting the small words.

eyebrow	high school	tongue-tied

Circle the compound word in each sentence below. Then write its separate parts on the line in front of the sentence.

_____ 1. The clowns put on their make-up and took their places.

_____ 2. During the art festival, the sidewalk was filled with people.

_____ 3. Hank Aaron hit 755 home runs during his long career.

_____ 4. My brother is the only left-handed person in our family.

_____ 5. Every Saturday, Carol baby-sits for her little cousin.

_____ 6. Terri screeched when she hit her funny bone on the desk.

_____ 7. The framework of the building looked like a giant steel web.

_____ 8. Huge waves smashed the beach at high tide.

_____ 9. Playing in the sunshine helps people stay healthy.

_____ 10. Last year, earthquakes hit the southern part of the state.

_____ 11. At camp, we slept in a cabin with bunk beds.

Plurals are words that name more than one. They are formed in several ways.

1. Add **-s** to most words.

   cab—cab**s**

2. Add **-es** to words that end in **s, x, sh, ch,** or **tch.**

   leash—leash**es**

3. Change **y** to **i** and add **-es** to words that end in a consonant plus **y.**

   duty—dut**ies**

4. Add **-s** to words that end in a vowel plus **y.**

   tray—tray**s**

5. Change **f** to **v** and add **-s** or **-es** to words that end in **f** or **fe.**

   leaf—lea**ves**

6. If a word ends in a consonant plus **o,** usually **-es** is added. If it ends in a vowel plus **o,** usually **-s** is added.

   potato—potato**es**   radio—radio**s**

On the first line after each word below, write the number of the sentence above that tells how to form its plural. On the second line, write the plural form.

1. sash ____ _____

2. tomato ____ _____

3. antler ____ _____

4. journey ____ _____

5. life ____ _____

6. victory ____ _____

7. chorus ____ _____

8. knife ____ _____

9. bully ____ _____

10. elbow ____ _____

11. calf ____ _____

12. rodeo ____ _____

13. ditch ____ _____

14. subway ____ _____

15. lasso ____ _____

16. guppy ____ _____

17. half ____ _____

18. ray ____ _____

19. mosquito ____ _____

20. tax ____ _____

21. diary ____ _____

22. zero ____ _____

23. variety ____ _____

24. melody ____ _____

The possessive form of a word shows ownership.

1. Add **'s** to words that name one person or animal.

2. Add an apostrophe (**'**) to plural words that end in **s**.

3. Add **'s** to plural words that do not end in **s**.

a mayor**'s** office

the rat**s'** nest

the geese**'s** feathers

In each sentence below, underline the phrase that can be rewritten to show possession. On the first line, write the number of the sentence above that tells how to make the word possessive. On the second line, write the possessive form.

1. Some babies can drink only the milk of goats. ____ _____

2. The homes of the mice were behind the warm stove. ____ _____

3. In many ways, the job of cowhands can be exciting. ____ _____

4. The cheers of the audience rang through the hall. ____ _____

5. Snow covered the tent of the explorer. ____ _____

6. The lines of the fishermen hung over the boat. ____ _____

7. All along the creek, dams of beavers could be seen. ____ _____

8. The ancestors of my friends came from Italy. ____ _____

9. The wool of the lamb was soft and fluffy. ____ _____

10. The crown of the king rested on a pillow next to the throne. ____ _____

11. I have to admire the courage of the policewomen. ____ _____

12. The expressions on the faces of the children showed their love of magic. ____ _____

13. Sara is the name of my cousin, too! ____ _____

14. The mother of the kittens was nowhere to be seen. ____ _____

The spellings of some words stay the same when a suffix is added.

ant + s = ants   clank + ing = clanking   leaf + y = leafy
arch + es = arches   mild + er = milder   slight + ly = slightly
bloom + ed = bloomed odd + est = oddest   peace + ful = peaceful

In each sentence below, underline the word whose spelling stayed the same when the suffix was added. Then write its base word on the line in front of the sentence.

_____ 1. Playing with fire can have a serious result.

_____ 2. The giraffe is the tallest animal in the world.

_____ 3. A mountain climber must always be alert for danger.

_____ 4. Jim Thorpe may have been the greatest athlete of all time.

_____ 5. Be sure the ashes from the fire are cold before we leave.

_____ 6. The helicopter hovered near the crash area.

_____ 7. Caleigh came home promptly for supper.

_____ 8. Lisa did not complain about the painful cut on her arm.

_____ 9. I am lonely when Dad is away on a business trip.

_____ 10. Mark was squirming in his seat through the entire speech.

_____ 11. Who put these pebbles in the bottom of the fishbowl?

_____ 12. The carton was stuffed into the closet.

_____ 13. The rocket blasted into space toward the planet Mars.

_____ 14. A sneaky fox got into the chicken house last night.

_____ 15. They say Bigfoot is seven feet tall and very hairy.

_____ 16. The best ride in the park is the super coaster.

_____ 17. My cousin is building a car for the soap box derby.

_____ 18. The river is rougher today than it was yesterday.

In some words, the final consonant is doubled before a suffix is added.

trip + p + ed = tripped   star + r + y = starry
plot + t + ing = plotting   hit + t + er = hitter

In each sentence below, underline the word in which the final consonant was doubled before the suffix was added. Then write its base word on the line in front of the sentence.

_____ 1. Denise is the best swimmer on her team.

_____ 2. Yesterday was sunny, but today it may rain.

_____ 3. Larry admitted that he broke the window.

_____ 4. Fortunately, the batter ducked out of the way of the fast ball.

_____ 5. Mapping out our trip across the country was fun.

_____ 6. My dog has a long, furry coat.

_____ 7. Skipping flat rocks across the water is easy.

_____ 8. The cookie cutter is in the bottom drawer.

_____ 9. Leo bragged all day about the fish he caught.

_____ 10. It was so foggy that I couldn't see the road.

_____ 11. A dripping faucet wastes a lot of water.

_____ 12. Since Lindsay never gives up, she can't be called a quitter.

_____ 13. The beavers dammed up the stream with small trees.

_____ 14. The dolphin flipped out of the water to catch the fish.

_____ 15. The topping on the cake was made of sugar, nuts, and syrup.

_____ 16. Frogs make funny noises at night.

_____ 17. As the candle burned down, the room became dimmer.

_____ 18. The bread popped out of the toaster and onto the floor.

When a word ends in a consonant plus **y**, the **y** is changed to **i** before a suffix is added.

dut~~y~~ + i + es = duties	sturd~~y~~ + i + est = sturdiest
bur~~y~~ + i + ed = buried	clums~~y~~ + i + ly = clumsily
ic~~y~~ + i + er = icier	beaut~~y~~ + i + ful = beautiful

In each sentence below, underline the word in which the **y** was changed to **i** before the suffix was added. Then write the word without its suffix on the line in front of the sentence.

_____ 1. No place is drier than the desert.

_____ 2. The football bounced crazily across the field.

_____ 3. The batteries in Denny's flashlight were dead.

_____ 4. Teresa shouted angrily when her brother pulled her hair.

_____ 5. My grandfather was the liveliest person at the picnic.

_____ 6. I can't decide which of the two movies was scarier.

_____ 7. Each time that river overflows, three counties are flooded.

_____ 8. These are the juiciest peaches I've ever eaten.

_____ 9. Who supplied the prizes at the Halloween party?

_____ 10. Many people live in large cities like New York.

_____ 11. I have never been thirstier than I was after that long hike.

_____ 12. Mr. Thompson seemed worried because the bus was late.

_____ 13. When Kay was done writing, she recopied her poem neatly.

_____ 14. I think the straw hat is more beautiful than the white one.

_____ 15. The kitten purrs happily when it is petted.

_____ 16. The bright fire made the room seem cozier.

_____ 17. Fresh corn is plentiful in summer.

_____ 18. That is the tiniest dog I've ever seen.

When a word ends in silent **e**, the **e** is usually dropped before a suffix is added.

welcom~~e~~ + ed = welcomed   cut~~e~~ + er = cuter   ros~~e~~ + y = rosy

judg~~e~~ + ing = judging   pur~~e~~ + est = purest

In each sentence below, underline the word in which the final silent **e** was dropped before the suffix was added. Then write its base word on the line in front of the sentence.

_____ 1. Is San Francisco closer to Portland or Los Angeles?

_____ 2. The North Star sparkled brightly in the night sky.

_____ 3. The family awoke before the smoky fire got too big.

_____ 4. The plane circled the airport for an hour before it landed.

_____ 5. The first problem on the page is usually the simplest.

_____ 6. Many whaling ships sailed out of New England ports.

_____ 7. The largest of the fifty states is Alaska.

_____ 8. Melanie raced through the park on her bike.

_____ 9. The soda was so bubbly that I began to sneeze.

_____ 10. The police were very puzzled about the robbery.

_____ 11. When you are leaving, remember to use the side door.

_____ 12. Why is the owl said to be the wisest animal?

_____ 13. The sidewalk is icy, so watch your step.

_____ 14. A giant spider was dangling over the table.

_____ 15. It feels good to get up on a breezy spring morning.

_____ 16. During a thunderstorm, it's safer to be inside than out.

_____ 17. Rhyming games are fun to play at parties.

_____ 18. Harriet Tubman was one of the bravest women in history.

1. The spelling of some base words is not changed before a suffix is added.
rugs

2. In some words, the final consonant is doubled before a suffix is added.
dragging

3. In some words, the final **y** is changed to **i** before a suffix is added.
prettiest

4. In most words with a final silent **e**, the **e** is dropped before a suffix is added.
moving

On the first line in front of each word below, write the number of the sentence above that tells how the suffix was added. On the second line, write the base word.

____ _____ 1. shady

____ _____ 2. wedding

____ _____ 3. peaceful

____ _____ 4. scarred

____ _____ 5. posters

____ _____ 6. nutty

____ _____ 7. abilities

____ _____ 8. rapidly

____ _____ 9. relating

____ _____ 10. boldest

____ _____ 11. jogging

____ _____ 12. chilly

____ _____ 13. satisfied

____ _____ 14. ordinarily

____ _____ 15. porches

____ _____ 16. freezer

____ _____ 17. knotted

____ _____ 18. thirsty

____ _____ 19. glider

____ _____ 20. barrelful

____ _____ 21. jealously

____ _____ 22. heroes

____ _____ 23. tanner

____ _____ 24. chirping

____ _____ 25. strained

____ _____ 26. necessarily

____ _____ 27. waded

____ _____ 28. soared

____ _____ 29. centuries

____ _____ 30. faintly

____ _____ 31. dripping

____ _____ 32. giggled

____ _____ 33. clumsiest

____ _____ 34. milder

____ _____ 35. clipping

____ _____ 36. sturdiest

Each of these prefixes means "not": **in-, non-, dis-,** and **un-**. The spelling of **in-** is changed to **im-** before words that begin with **m, b,** or **p.**

in | complete   **non | living**   **dis | agree**   **un | welcome**
im | patient

The prefixes **un-** and **dis-** can also mean "the opposite of" the word to which they are added.

un | cover   **dis | connect**

Complete each sentence below by adding one of the above prefixes to each incomplete word.

1. There are very few vegetables that Connie _____likes.

2. Miguel sent me a message written in _____visible ink.

3. The old coin was _____like any other I'd ever seen.

4. The campers could not drink the water because it was _____pure.

5. I was amazed when the magician made the elephant _____appear.

6. We arrived at the meeting late because we took an _____direct route.

7. Aunt Martha paid us an _____expected visit yesterday.

8. Lan became _____patient when her car would not start.

9. If you _____agree with the new rule, tell me your reasons.

10. The train traveled _____stop from Washington, DC, to New York City.

11. It is _____polite to eat food with a knife.

12. Gerry had only one _____correct answer on his test.

13. Pioneers are thrilled with thoughts of the _____known.

14. I like the taste of _____fat milk.

15. To me, believing in ghosts is _____sense.

16. The _____complete game will be finished next week.

17. How can I _____lock the door if I've lost the key?

18. Kevin was _____pleased with his science grade.

The prefix **fore-** means "in front."

The prefix **sub-** means "under" or "below."

fore | foot

sub | way

The prefix **pre-** means "before."

The prefix **inter-** means "between" or "among."

pre | pay

inter | state

Each sentence below contains a word with the prefix **fore-, pre-, sub-,** or **inter-.**
Underline the word and draw a line after the prefix. Then write its definition on
the line.

1. If you preheat the oven, it will be hot when you put in the cake.

   _____

2. The preview of next week's show looked exciting.

   _____

3. Temperatures in Florida are almost never subfreezing.

   _____

4. The sun is not as hot in the forenoon as it is after twelve.

   _____

5. The subsoil was rockier than the rich earth on the surface.

   _____

6. These frozen vegetables have been precooked and only need to be warmed up.

   _____

7. Some people believe they can foretell the weather by watching caterpillars.

   _____

8. A subtitle sometimes gives a clue to what a book is about.

   _____

9. Most countries have strong laws about international trade.

   _____

The prefix **mis-** means "wrong."   The prefix **re-** means "back" or "again."

mis | print   **re | paid**   **re | build**

In the list below, circle each word in which **mis-** or **re-** is a prefix. Underline the base word.

repay	mister	restart	replaced	misfortune
misty	recopy	misstep	misfired	misspelled
reprint	reader	reclaim	misjudged	repainted
reason	refill	recounted	relocated	misunderstand

Complete each sentence below by writing one of the words circled above on the line.

1. Nick took the paint set from the shelf, checked the price, and quickly

   _____ it.

2. Once the car stopped, Jody could not _____ it.

3. A word is _____ on page seven of my math book.

4. The tourist did not know how to _____ Charlene's kindness.

5. If you speak slowly, no one will _____ what you're saying.

6. Last summer, the schoolrooms were _____ a bright color.

7. After lunch, _____ the pitcher with more fruit punch.

8. The center fielder _____ the fly ball, and it dropped to the ground.

9. Lisa had to _____ her report after she dropped it in a puddle.

10. Alfredo had the _____ of breaking his leg in a football game.

11. The farmer _____ the beehives farther from the house.

12. Wendy went to the bus station to _____ her lost coat.

13. If you take just one _____, you could easily fall from the roof.

14. When the pirate's cannon _____, the little ship escaped.

15. Bill _____ his change after he left the store.

Each of these suffixes means "the action of doing" or "the state of being": **-ion, -sion, -ation,** and **-ition.**

perfect**ion**   persua**sion**   explan**ation**   add**ition**

After each word below, write its base word. Use a dictionary to check the spelling.

1. prevention _____

2. observation _____

3. direction _____

4. exploration _____

5. suggestion _____

6. action _____

7. invitation _____

8. decoration _____

9. location _____

10. introduction _____

The suffix **-ment** means
"the action of doing" pay**ment**
"the state of being" accomplish**ment**
"a thing that" state**ment**

The suffix **-ness** means
"the state of being" dark**ness**

Complete each sentence below by adding one of the suffixes on this page to the word in front of the sentence. Write the new word on the line.

settle   1. Jamestown was the first _____ in this country.

bright   2. The sudden _____ of the sun hurt my eyes.

protect   3. A porcupine has excellent natural _____.

add   4. The Bowers family just put an _____ on their house.

imagine   5. Sometimes Jackson lets his _____ run away with him.

confuse   6. The flood caused a lot of _____ in the town.

improve   7. Roni knows that her spelling needs _____.

strange   8. There was a _____ about the house that scared Ben.

collect   9. My brother has a large _____ of CDs.

admire   10. People have great _____ for President Lincoln.

The suffix **-ful** means
    "full of"   care**ful**
    "the amount that fills" cup**ful**

The suffix **-less** means
    "without"   care**less**

Complete the paragraph below by writing **-ful** or **-less** on each line.

Have you ever thought about being trapped in a room_____ of panthers? What would you do if you had a house_____ of tigers? Can you imagine being in such a hope_____ situation? If you were the fear_____ Gunter Gebel-Williams, you'd have had no problem at all. You'd simply tell the growling but respect_____ cats to sit down. And they would! Gunther Gebel-Williams was the world's most famous animal trainer. He didn't work with tooth_____ old animals that couldn't hurt him. And his cats certainly weren't play_____ little kittens, either. Gebel-Williams trained power_____ panthers and tigers. They could have eaten him in a big mouth_____. One care_____ mistake by Gebel-Williams could mean pain_____ injuries or even death. He was a care_____ man, though. And that made him success_____. To his other traits, he added a huge cup_____ of courage. He always personally gave his cats food by the hand_____. So Gebel-Williams got to know them. He knew them well enough to wear a live leopard for a shawl! Gunther Gebel-Williams performed to the end_____ applause of circus fans all over the world.

Write each word with the suffix **-ful** in the correct column.

"full of"		**"the amount that fills"**	
_____	_____	_____	_____
_____	_____	_____	_____
_____	_____		_____

Each of these suffixes means "a person who": **-er** and **-or.**

The suffix **-ist** also means "a person who." It tells that the person has something to do with the base word.

paint**er**   visit**or**   violin**ist**

Make a new word by adding **-er, -or,** or **-ist** to each word below. Write the new word on the line. You may need to change the spelling of a base word before adding a suffix.

1. explore _____

2. art   _____

3. report   _____

4. science _____

5. box   _____

6. speak   _____

7. weave   _____

8. act   _____

9. special   _____

10. swim   _____

11. invent   _____

12. entertain _____

Complete the crossword puzzle by using the new words above.

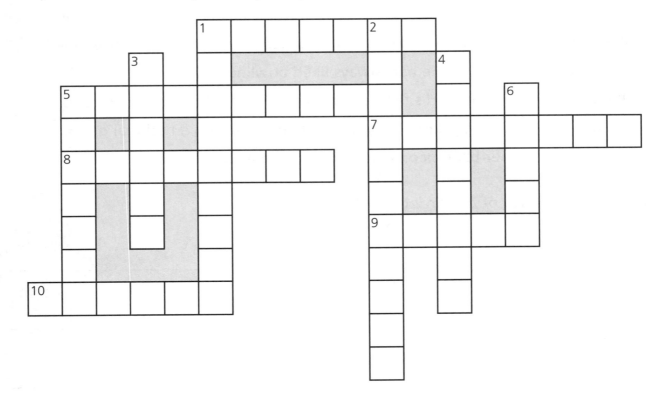

ACROSS

1. A _____ talks to someone else.
5. A _____ does particular tasks.
7. An _____ travels to unknown places.
8. An _____ creates new things.
9. An _____ plays a part in the movies.
10. An _____ works with paintings.

DOWN

1. A _____ may study nature.
2. An _____ performs for others in public.
3. A _____ makes rugs, baskets, etc.
4. A _____ gathers news.
5. A _____ moves through the water.
6. A _____ fights with fists for sport.

Suffixes **-er, -or,** and **-ist**   43

The suffixes **-able** and **-ible** mean "able to" and "able to be done."

accept**able**   forc**ible**

The suffix **-al** means "of or belonging to" or "the action of."

comic**al**   dismiss**al**

In the paragraph below, circle each word with the suffix **-able, -ible,** or **-al.**

Last weekend, I had a remarkable experience. My friends and I went bowling. Right after our arrival, we rented bowling shoes and went to our lane. Two people came to the lane next to ours, and it was noticeable that the man was moving slowly and carefully. I soon realized that he was blind, but that was not recognizable at first. In a few moments, the two people were putting up a railing made of light metal. Then this admirable man began to bowl! To guide him down the alley, he ran his right hand along the railing. His shot was respectable even for a person who could see. I found out later that the man had been hurt as a soldier. His personal refusal to let blindness slow him down was amazing. He had always liked bowling so it seemed natural and sensible to continue. His first railing was experimental, but now he and his wife go bowling regularly. They have also helped form a national group that supports other blind people who want to be active in sports.

Write the base words of the circled words.

_____   _____   _____

_____   _____   _____

_____   _____   _____

_____   _____   _____

The suffix **-y** means		The suffix **-ly** means	
"like"	storm**y**	"like"	brother**ly**
"full of"	salt**y**	"each" or "every"	year**ly**
"the state of being"	jealous**y**	"in a way that is"	quiet**ly**

Complete each sentence below by adding **-y** or **-ly** to a word in the word box.

WORD BOX

rock	soap	swamp	snow	difficult
home	night	perfect	silent	week
loud	fish	shy	honest	friend

1. The old wooden dock had a _____ smell.

2. Brad used a bucket of _____ water to clean the car.

3. The beautiful butterfly perched _____ on the flower.

4. Lee eagerly awaits her _____ paycheck each Friday.

5. The little log cabin was very _____ inside.

6. Caitlin smiled _____ for the camera.

7. The fireworks thundered _____ and lit up the sky.

8. Some TV shows are on _____ and some only once a week.

9. With much _____, Brett used crutches to climb the stairs.

10. I always like to be the first person to walk through a _____ field.

11. Mr. Maggio gave me a _____ smile when we were introduced.

12. The _____ path made hiking difficult.

13. Mike showed his _____ when he returned the lost wallet to its owner.

14. After the heavy rains, the field was too _____ to walk through.

15. Kelly can imitate _____ the calls made by different birds.

The suffix **-ish** means
"like"   child**ish**
"somewhat"   brown**ish**

The suffix **-ous** means
"full of"   glori**ous**

Circle the suffix in each word below. Then write the base word on the line.

1. mysterious _____

2. smallish _____

3. poisonous _____

4. dangerous _____

5. longish _____

6. sickish _____

7. adventurous _____

8. humorous _____

9. marvelous _____

10. famous _____

11. pinkish _____

12. tallish _____

Complete each sentence below with one of the words from the list above.

1. The game was _____, but we got home in time for dinner.

2. A sign warned drivers of a _____ curve in the road ahead.

3. Just before sunset the sky glowed with a beautiful _____ color.

4. Be sure to keep _____ items out of the reach of small children.

5. Our new car is _____ and doesn't use much gas.

6. The _____ noise outside our tent kept us awake all night.

7. We laughed at the _____ story Mr. Wilson told.

8. The _____ people should stand in the back row, not the front.

9. The astronauts returned safely from their _____ trip into space.

10. Sometimes I daydream about being a _____ actor.

11. The way the team came from behind and won was _____.

12. Ms. Newton still felt _____ after she came home from the hospital.

Prefixes		Suffixes		
in-, im-, dis-, un-	sub-	-ion, -sion, -ation, -ition	-y, -ly	-less
pre-	inter-	-er, -or	-ment	-ist
fore-	re-	-able, -ible	-ness	-al
mis-		-ous	-ful	-ish

Complete each sentence by adding one of the prefixes above to the word below the line.

1. I find it a help to _____ my work for each coming week.
   plan

2. Jesse bumped his _____ on the car door.
   head

3. The _____ disappeared into a dark tunnel.
   way

4. I will not be able to _____ you until next week.
   pay

5. Large _____ highways connect the Atlantic and Pacific coasts.
   state

6. Please do not _____ the library books.
   use

7. Friends can _____ with each other and still be friends.
   agree

Complete each sentence by adding one of the suffixes above to the word below the line.

1. The _____ filled the bottle with red pills.
   drug

2. Tiana's _____ kept her home for ten days.
   ill

3. My latest _____ seems to be working.
   invent

4. The rug will not fit unless the _____ of the room is correct.
   measure

5. The _____ vase fell and is now in hundreds of pieces.
   break

6. The _____ radioed his position to the Coast Guard.
   sail

7. Fog has caused the late _____ of Jenna's plane.
   arrive

Prefixes		Suffixes		
in-, im-, dis-, un-	sub-	-ion, -sion, -ation, -ition	-y, -ly	-less
pre-	inter-	-er, -or	-ment	-ist
fore-	re-	-able, -ible	-ness	-al
mis-		-ous	-ful	-ish

In the paragraph below, circle each word that contains one of the prefixes or suffixes above.

Ansel Adams is widely regarded as the father of modern photography. Everyone recognizes his black-and-white pictures of the Sierra Nevada Mountains in California. Adams was born in San Francisco in 1902. At first he went to a traditional school, but he was unhappy in the classroom and misbehaved. His parents decided to home school him, and they encouraged his enjoyment in exploring the outdoors. In 1915, an exhibition about the Panama Canal captured his interest. He revisited it day after day. But it was a vacation in 1916 that foretold his future. That year the Adams family went to Yosemite National Park, and his parents gave Ansel his first camera. Although Adams once thought he would be a pianist, it was soon clear that the camera was his future.

On each line below, write one of the circled words. Then write another word you know with the same prefix or suffix.

1. _____

2. _____

3. _____

4. _____

5. _____

6. _____

7. _____

8. _____

9. _____

10. _____

Underline the prefixes and the suffixes in the words below. Then write the base words on the lines.

1. discontinue _____

2. noticeable _____

3. subplot _____

4. traveler _____

5. stylish _____

6. observation _____

7. mispronounce _____

8. fearless _____

9. interstate _____

10. jealousy _____

11. confusion _____

12. unaware _____

13. youthful _____

14. repack _____

15. scarcely _____

16. foresee _____

17. childish _____

18. collector _____

19. violinist _____

20. humorous _____

21. incomplete _____

22. protection _____

23. juicy _____

24. painless _____

25. preview _____

26. natural _____

27. eagerness _____

28. nonsense _____

29. impatient _____

30. addition _____

31. payment _____

32. forenoon _____

33. sensible _____

34. unequal _____

35. nonbreakable _____

36. unselfish _____

37. subtropical _____

38. indirectly _____

39. forecaster _____

40. disrespectful _____

41. interaction _____

42. immovable _____

Prefixes   in-, im-, dis-, un-, pre-, fore-, mis-, sub-, inter-, re-

Suffixes   -ion, -sion, -ation, -ition, -ment, -ness, -ful, -less,
              -er, -or, -ist, -able, -ible, -al, -y, -ly, -ish, -ous

In the paragraph below, underline each word that contains one of the prefixes or suffixes above.

I was impatiently awaiting the arrival of our vacation. It was going to be my first trip to the ocean. We left at dawn one July morning. There was no confusion. We had finished packing the night before. As soon as I got in the car, my imagination started working. The pictures in my mind were like a movie preview. First I thought of foamy waves crashing onto the beach. Then I thought of an uneven stretch of sand. I imagined the boardwalk. Often I stopped the action in my mind. Then I could look at it like a picture an artist had painted. It was all wonderful! I even pictured being a sailor on a submarine. I discontinued my daydreaming when we got to the shore. To my astonishment, the beach and the ocean were more beautiful than I had thought. Even though I'm home again, I'm still a daydreamer. Now I replay in my mind movies of the good time I really had.

Write the base word for each underlined word above.

1. _____

2. _____

3. _____

4. _____

5. _____

6. _____

7. _____

8. _____

9. _____

10. _____

11. _____

12. _____

13. _____

14. _____

15. _____

16. _____

17. _____

18. _____

On each line below, write the contraction formed by the two words.

1. they will _____

2. she is _____

3. I am _____

4. what is _____

5. we had _____

6. there is _____

7. he has _____

8. they are _____

9. you have _____

10. do not _____

Draw a line to connect two words that form a compound word. Then write the new compound word on the line.

spring	print	1. _____
ever	sight	2. _____
eye	spoon	3. _____
week	born	4. _____
home	time	5. _____
foot	made	6. _____
sun	end	7. _____
new	green	8. _____
tea	rise	9. _____

Rewrite each phrase to show possession.

1. the room of the guests _____

2. the park of the children _____

3. the scales of a butcher _____

4. the tricks of the dolphins _____

5. the treasure of a pirate _____

6. the necks of the oxen _____

7. the instruments of the musicians _____

8. the spacesuit of an astronaut _____

9. the whiskers of the mice _____

1. The spelling of some words is not changed before a suffix is added.
2. In some words, the final consonant is doubled before a suffix is added.
3. In some words, the final **y** is changed to **i** before a suffix is added.
4. In most words with a final silent **e**, the **e** is dropped before a suffix is added.

On the line in front of each word, write the number of the sentence above that tells how the ending was added to the word. On the line after each word, write its base word.

____ 1. abilities _____   ____ 8. soapy _____

____ 2. thriller _____   ____ 9. hissing _____

____ 3. boiled _____   ____ 10. envied _____

____ 4. foggy _____   ____ 11. gripping _____

____ 5. smokiest _____   ____ 12. juicy _____

____ 6. dozing _____   ____ 13. winner _____

____ 7. supplies _____   ____ 14. tamest _____

After each word, write its word parts in the correct column.

	Prefix	Base Word	Suffix
1. impatiently	_____	_____	_____
2. returnable	_____	_____	_____
3. unlikeable	_____	_____	_____
4. misstatement	_____	_____	_____
5. disorderly	_____	_____	_____
6. international	_____	_____	_____
7. unsuccessful	_____	_____	_____
8. refinisher	_____	_____	_____
9. nonpoisonous	_____	_____	_____
10. dislocation	_____	_____	_____

Each syllable in a word contains one vowel sound. To find out the number of syllables in a word, count the number of vowel sounds you hear.

Below each picture, write the number of syllables you hear in the picture name.

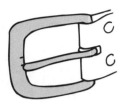    

_____ _____ _____ _____ _____

_____ _____ _____ _____ _____

On each line write the number of syllables you hear in the word.

____ 1. roam

____ 2. librarian

____ 3. area

____ 4. olive

____ 5. uneasily

____ 6. bruise

____ 7. hamburger

____ 8. pause

____ 9. territory

____ 10. gradual

____ 11. discovery

____ 12. necessary

____ 13. skeleton

____ 14. envelope

____ 15. wheat

____ 16. festival

____ 17. society

____ 18. forehead

____ 19. oxygen

____ 20. poet

____ 21. vinegar

____ 22. rhyme

____ 23. doubt

____ 24. heaven

____ 25. lonely

____ 26. forever

____ 27. ache

____ 28. kneel

____ 29. elegant

____ 30. throughout

____ 31. kennel

____ 32. geography

____ 33. improvement

____ 34. pronunciation

____ 35. experience

____ 36. responsibility

____ 37. unexpected

____ 38. journey

____ 39. conversation

____ 40. imagination

When you are writing, you may need to divide a word at the end of a line. You must divide between syllables.

1. If a word contains a double consonant, divide **between** the double consonant.

    spar | row

2. If two unlike consonants come between two vowels, divide **between** the consonants.

    lan | tern

3. If a consonant comes between two vowels and the first vowel is short, divide **after** the consonant.

    liz | ard

4. If a consonant comes between two vowels and the first vowel is long, divide **before** the consonant.

    pu | pil

5. If a word ends in **le** and a consonant comes before **le,** divide **before** the consonant.

    an | kle

6. If two vowels come together in a word and each vowel stands for one sound, divide **between** the vowels.

    li | on

On the line in front of each word, write the number of the sentence that tells how the word is divided. Then draw a line to divide the word into syllables.

____ 1. cabin

____ 2. tunnel

____ 3. jungle

____ 4. silence

____ 5. twenty

____ 6. shiver

____ 7. cruel

____ 8. jingle

____ 9. flutter

____ 10. trial

____ 11. patient

____ 12. captain

____ 13. metal

____ 14. private

____ 15. cider

____ 16. native

____ 17. sample

____ 18. canyon

____ 19. cocoa

____ 20. legend

____ 21. giant

____ 22. tangle

____ 23. salad

____ 24. costume

____ 25. collapse

____ 26. future

____ 27. velvet

____ 28. clipper

____ 29. column

____ 30. sprinkle

____ 31. science

____ 32. bamboo

____ 33. poet

____ 34. success

____ 35. human

____ 36. marble

____ 37. clumsy

____ 38. monarch

____ 39. tremble

____ 40. soda

1. Words that contain a consonant blend or a consonant digraph are usually not divided between the letters that make up the blend or digraph.

ze | **bra**   buck | et

2. If a prefix or a suffix is added to a base word, it usually forms a separate syllable.

un | lock   sail | **or**

3. In a compound word, divide between the words that make up the compound word.

bee | hive

On the line in front of each word below, write the number of the sentence above that tells how the word is divided. (Sometimes more than one number could be used.) Then divide the word into syllables. On the line after the word, write the letter of the correct definition.

_____ 1. preview _____   a. a place where medicine is sold

_____ 2. airport _____   b. terrible

_____ 3. dreadful _____   c. a black leopard

_____ 4. panther _____   d. a person who raises cattle, sheep, or horses

_____ 5. highway _____   e. soft and light

_____ 6. replace _____   f. to put back

_____ 7. drugstore _____   g. a person who buys and sells goods

_____ 8. fluffy _____   h. a place where planes land and take off

_____ 9. rancher _____   i. to see ahead of time

_____ 10. merchant _____   j. a main road

Divide the words in each group into syllables. On the line in front of each word, write the number of the word in the box that is divided in the same way. (Sometimes more than one number can be used.)

1. Double consonants—mit | ten
2. Unlike consonants—hun | ger
3. Short vowel/consonant/vowel—rap | id
4. Long vowel/consonant/vowel—ci | der
5. Consonant before **le**—mar | ble
6. Between two vowels—po | et

_____ 1. habit

_____ 2. collect

_____ 3. couple

_____ 4. label

_____ 5. member

_____ 6. heaven

_____ 7. real

_____ 8. turtle

_____ 9. runner

_____ 10. dial

_____ 11. beaver

_____ 12. timber

_____ 13. finish

_____ 14. creature

_____ 15. beyond

_____ 16. bacon

_____ 17. castle

_____ 18. certain

_____ 19. crayon

_____ 20. lemon

_____ 21. riot

_____ 22. puzzle

_____ 23. cover

_____ 24. picnic

7. Blend or digraph—pro | gram, thick | et
8. Prefix or suffix—un | like, wood | en
9. Compound word—bull | dog

_____ 1. sunshine

_____ 2. lonely

_____ 3. prefix

_____ 4. daylight

_____ 5. leafy

_____ 6. redo

_____ 7. twister

_____ 8. schoolroom

_____ 9. disgrace

_____ 10. nowhere

_____ 11. mouthful

_____ 12. somehow

_____ 13. flashlight

_____ 14. breathless

_____ 15. bushel

_____ 16. firefly

_____ 17. pancake

_____ 18. orchard

_____ 19. speechless

_____ 20. railroad

_____ 21. eyebrow

_____ 22. unload

_____ 23. windshield

_____ 24. misspell

To alphabetize words that begin with the same letter or letters, find the first letter in each word that is different. Then put the words in alphabetical order according to these letters.

n**o**rth	nail
n**a**il	neck
n**i**ght	night
n**e**ck	north

Number the words in each group in alphabetical order.

___ dozen   ___ leave   ___ trainer   ___ forty

___ dolphin   ___ lean   ___ trail   ___ forth

___ dock   ___ learn   ___ track   ___ formed

___ doubt   ___ leash   ___ trains   ___ fortune

Complete the alphabetical list below with the words in the word box.

WORD BOX

goldfish	jingle	imagine	backyard
disappear	quarrel	visible	often
office	operate	quarter	young
imitate	disease	golden	immediate
operator	background	jigsaw	visitor

1. _____

2. backward

3. _____

4. _____

5. disappoint

6. _____

7. disgrace

8. _____

9. _____

10. imaginary

11. imagination

12. _____

13. _____

14. _____

15. jiggle

16. _____

17. _____

18. offer

19. _____

20. official

21. _____

22. open

23. _____

24. _____

25. opinion

26. quack

27. _____

28. _____

29. violin

30. _____

31. _____

32. _____

33. youth

Think of a dictionary as having three parts: front, middle, and back.

Front	Middle	Back
Words beginning with **a, b, c, d, e, f,** and **g**	Words beginning with **h, i, j, k, l, m, n, o,** and **p**	Words beginning with **q, r, s, t, u, v, w, x, y,** and **z**

When you look for a word in a dictionary, decide which part it is in. Then open the dictionary to that part. This will save you time in looking for a word.

In which part of a dictionary are the following words found? On each line, write **front, middle,** or **back.**

1. moan _____

2. web _____

3. canary _____

4. quiver _____

5. former _____

6. kettle _____

7. zipper _____

8. alert _____

9. navy _____

10. tickle _____

11. gesture _____

12. seek _____

13. barge _____

14. van _____

15. kangaroo _____

16. pinch _____

17. harvest _____

18. dignity _____

19. yelp _____

20. law _____

21. olive _____

The words in a dictionary are listed in alphabetical order.

Write five more words in alphabetical order that would be found in each section of a dictionary.

Front	Middle	Back
_____	_____	_____
_____	_____	_____
_____	_____	_____
_____	_____	_____
_____	_____	_____

The two boldface words at the top of a dictionary page are called **guide words.** The word on the left tells the first word on a page. The one on the right tells the last word on a page. Words that come alphabetically between the two guide words are found on that page.

table	604	tale	talk	605	tap
tape	606	teach	teacher	607	tell

Look at the guide words for the four dictionary pages shown above. On each line, write the number of the page on which the word is found.

_____ 1. tank

_____ 2. team

_____ 3. tag

_____ 4. tasty

_____ 5. tall

_____ 6. tea

_____ 7. tack

_____ 8. taught

_____ 9. tame

_____ 10. tear

_____ 11. task

_____ 12. tan

_____ 13. taxi

_____ 14. tail

_____ 15. tease

_____ 16. tangle

_____ 17. tailor

_____ 18. teeth

_____ 19. taste

_____ 20. taken

After each pair of guide words, underline the words that would appear on that page.

1. **ledge—lid**   leave   lie   level   lift

2. **vein—vine**   van   view   violin   village

3. **ill—inch**   immediate   impatient   indeed   idea

4. **dough—drawn**   dream   doubt   dozen   dragon

5. **east—effort**   eaten   edge   ease   effect

6. **modern—month**   moment   monkey   mood   model

7. **north—now**   notch   noon   nowhere   notice

8. **pole—porch**   poke   port   poppy   polite

9. **quarrel—quick**   quart   question   quack   quite

10. **grape—green**   great   grand   greet   grasp

The words defined in a dictionary are called entry words. They are always listed alphabetically. Usually they are also written in dark type and divided into syllables.

Entry Word →

poke 478 **remarkable**

poke /pōk/, **1.** to push a person or thing with something pointed: *She poked herself with a pencil.* **2.** to push or pry into things: *Don't poke into other people's business.* **3.** a pushing or poking. **4.** to move in a slow, lazy way: *Jeff poked along on his way to school.* 1, 2, 4 *verb*, **poked, pok•ing;** 3 *noun*.

pol•ka /pōl' kə or pō' kə/, **1.** a lively dance. **2.** the music for this dance. *noun, plural* **pol•kas.**

prowl /proul/, **1.** to move about quietly and secretly as if hunting for something. **2.** to wander. **3.** a prowling. 1, 2 *verb*, 3 *noun*.

quart /kwôrt/, **1.** a liquid measure equal to one fourth of a gallon: *a quart of oil.* **2.** a dry measure equal to one eighth of a peck: *a quart of strawberries. noun.*

Queens /kwēnz/, a borough of New York City, east of Brooklyn on Long Island. *noun.*

quiv•er¹ /kwiv' ər/, **1.** to shake; to tremble: *Although the man escaped from the burning house, he still quivered in fear.* **2.** a shaking or trembling: *The quiver of the tree branch startled me.* 1 *verb*, 2 *noun*.

quiv•er² /kwiv' ər/, a case for holding arrows. *noun.*

race•track /rās' trak/, a round or oval area of ground laid out for racing. *noun.*

rat /rat/, **1.** a gnawing animal that looks like a mouse but is larger, with gray, brown, black, or white fur. **2.** a mean person. *noun.*

read•er /rē' dər/, **1.** a person who reads. **2.** a book for learning or practicing reading. *noun.*

reef /rēf/, a ridge of rocks or sand at or near the surface of the water. *noun.*

re•mark•a•ble /ri mär' kə bəl/, worthy of being noticed, unusual: *The new sculpture in front of the museum is remarkable. adjective.*

← Entry Word

1. How many entry words are shown? _____

2. How many entry words begin with **q**? _____

3. How many entry words have only one syllable? _____

4. Which entry word has four syllables? _____

5. Which entry word begins with a capital letter? _____

6. Which entry words have endings added to them? _____

7. Which entry word is a compound word? _____

8. Which spelling has two entries? _____

9. Which entry word has two pronunciations? _____

Not all words are listed as entry words in a dictionary. If endings or suffixes have been added to words, the words are often included with the entry of the base word.

ac•cuse /ə kūz´/, to blame for being or doing something wrong: *Our neighbors accused me of breaking the window.* verb, **ac•cused, ac•cus•ing.**

cen•tur•y /sen´ chər ē/, a period of 100 years. *noun, plural* **cen•tur•ies.**

child /chīld/, **1.** a baby. **2.** a young boy or girl. **3.** a son or daughter. *noun, plural* **chil•dren.**

eat /ēt/, **1.** to chew and swallow food. **2.** to have a meal: *We ate at six o'clock.* **3.** to wear away; to destroy; *The rust ate a hole in the bottom of the car door.* verb, **ate, eat•en, eat•ing.**

The words below may not be listed as entry words in a dictionary. On the line after each one, write the entry word that would include it.

1. freer _____
2. located _____
3. trimmest _____
4. quitting _____
5. waddled _____
6. abilities _____
7. fittest _____
8. heroes _____
9. readier _____
10. mapped _____
11. expresses _____
12. boring _____
13. unhappier _____
14. rarest _____
15. imitated _____

16. owing _____
17. drier _____
18. confused _____
19. noticing _____
20. youths _____
21. blamed _____
22. jolliest _____
23. circled _____
24. dozing _____
25. separated _____
26. valleys _____
27. oldest _____
28. measuring _____
29. kidded _____
30. overgrowing _____

In a dictionary, the pronunciation of each word is shown after the entry word. The letters or symbols used represent the sound heard in the word. The pronunciation key below is like the one found in a dictionary.

Pronunciation Key

a cat	ā cake	ä father	ch chin	e red	ē see	ėr her	
g get	i big	ī ride	j jump	ng ring	o stop	ō hope	
ô talk	oi noise	ou out	s sit	sh shall	th thank		
th then	u cut	u̇ put	ü rule	yū cute	zh pleasure		
ə about, spoken, giraffe, police, picture				z rose			

After each respelling below, write the key word from the pronunciation key above that tells how the underlined letter or letters are pronounced.

1. cho̅z _____
2. dout _____
3. rông _____
4. grip _____
5. helth _____
6. not _____
7. e̅z _____
8. flap _____
9. tho̅ _____
10. rij _____
11. hu̇d _____
12. se̅l _____

13. jüs _____
14. blėrt _____
15. dusk _____
16. pān _____
17. kyūb _____
18. trash _____
19. left _____
20. hôk _____
21. rīm _____
22. chois _____
23. mug _____
24. ärch _____

Use the pronunciation key to decide which respelling tells how to pronounce the word at the left. Circle the correct respelling.

1. **ghost**	jōst	fōst	gōst	gost
2. **ache**	āch	āk	ak	ach
3. **height**	hāt	heft	hit	hīt
4. **scene**	skēn	sān	sen	sēn
5. **lodge**	log	lōg	loj	loch

Every dictionary includes in its pronunciation key a symbol that looks like an upside down **e**. This symbol is called a schwa. It stands for the vowel sound often heard in a syllable that is not stressed. Each vowel can have the sound of the schwa. The pronunciation key gives words to help pronounce it.

sofa	barrel	dolphin	anchor	column
sō´fə	bar´əl	dol´fən	ang´kər	kol´əm

In each word below, circle the vowel that stands for the schwa sound.

1. upper
2. purpose
3. wizard
4. council
5. doubtful

6. tailor
7. temper
8. zebra
9. perform
10. canyon

11. disease
12. success
13. siren
14. effect
15. capture

16. bacon
17. support
18. ashore
19. fossil
20. canoe

On the line in front of each respelling, write the letter of its word.

____ 1. plā´ər
____ 2. prə nouns´
____ 3. pān´tər
____ 4. pärt´nər
____ 5. peb´əl
____ 6. pər fôrm´
____ 7. pat´ərn
____ 8. pər swād´
____ 9. prə vīd´
____ 10. pėr´pəs

a. perform
b. persuade
c. partner
d. player
e. purpose
f. pattern
g. provide
h. painter
i. pronounce
j. pebble

____ 11. sə lüt´
____ 12. shep´ərd
____ 13. sə plī´
____ 14. stub´ərn
____ 15. sam´pəl
____ 16. shel´tər
____ 17. shuf´əl
____ 18. sput´ər
____ 19. sim´pəl
____ 20. sim´bəl

k. sample
l. sputter
m. shelter
n. salute
o. simple
p. supply
q. shuffle
r. symbol
s. stubborn
t. shepherd

If a word has more than one syllable, one of the syllables is usually stressed more than the others. In a dictionary, an accent mark (ʹ) is placed next to the syllable with the most stress.

puppet	antlers	caboose	celery	magician
pupʹ it	antʹ lərz	kə büsʹ	selʹ ər ē	mə jishʹ ən

Each word below is divided into syllables. Put an accent mark after the syllable with the most stress.

1. im prove

2. kan ga roo

3. mod ern

4. a corn

5. vol ca no

6. bam boo

7. de vel op

8. med i cal

9. fau cet

10. sat el lite

11. pro nounce

12. en ter tain

13. pi o neer

14. wis dom

15. ex am ine

16. op po site

17. com mit tee

18. de fend

19. pat tern

20. to ma to

21. grad u al

On the first line in front of each word, write the number of syllables heard in it. On the second line, write the number of the syllable with the most stress.

_____ _____ 1. disappoint

_____ _____ 2. journey

_____ _____ 3. imitate

_____ _____ 4. interrupt

_____ _____ 5. musician

_____ _____ 6. accept

_____ _____ 7. messenger

_____ _____ 8. useless

_____ _____ 9. foreign

_____ _____ 10. introduce

_____ _____ 11. pacific

_____ _____ 12. hesitate

In words with more than one syllable, more than one syllable may be stressed. In a dictionary, a dark accent mark (ˊ) is placed next to the syllable with the most stress. A light accent mark (ˊ) is placed next to the syllable which is also stressed but not as much.

alligator   flashlight

alˊ ə gāˊ tər   flashˊ lītˊ

Each word below is divided into syllables. Put a dark accent mark (ˊ) after the syllable with the most stress. Put a light accent mark (ˊ) after the syllable which is also stressed but not as much.

1. hand writ ing
2. bas ket ball
3. far a way
4. un dis turbed
5. vi o lin
6. moon light
7. eye brow
8. pi o neer

9. rec tan gle
10. in for ma tion
11. ham burg er
12. rep re sent
13. frame work
14. dec o rate
15. en ter tain
16. no bod y

17. an ces tor
18. con ver sa tion
19. card board
20. ant eat er
21. sit u a tion
22. es ca la tor
23. dic tion ar y
24. nec es sar y

The phonetic respellings of some of the above words are given below. Add both the dark and light accent marks to each one. Then write the normal spelling on the line.

1. rep ri zent _____
2. kärd bôrd _____
3. en tər tān _____
4. ham bėr gər _____
5. nes ə ser ē _____
6. ī brou _____

7. pī ə nir _____
8. dik shə ner ē _____
9. rek tang gəl _____
10. frām wėrk _____
11. kon vər sā shən _____
12. an ses tər _____

Read the pairs of words below. Notice the shift of accent in the word with the suffix. When the suffix **-al, -ial, -ic, -ical, -ian, -ious,** or **-ity** is added to a word, the primary accent shifts to the syllable before the suffix.

mu´ sic   mu si´ cian   her´ o   he ro´ ic

The shift of accent in a word with a suffix often results in a vowel change.

po´ et /pō´ it/   po et´ ic /pō et´ ik/

col´ o ny /kol´ ə nē/   co lo´ ni al /kə lō´ nē əl/

Each word below is divided into syllables. Put a dark accent mark after the syllable with the most stress. Then circle any vowel that sounds different when the suffix is added and the accent shifts.

1. e qual   e qual i ty   9. mag net   mag net ic
2. mys ter y   mys ter i ous   10. cour age   cou ra geous
3. or i gin   o rig i nal   11. pres i dent   pres i den tial
4. mem or y   me mo ri al   12. li brar y   li brar i an
5. his tor y   his to ri cal   13. cur i ous   cur i os i ty
6. al pha bet   al pha bet i cal   14. mi cro scope   mi cro scop ic
7. ac ci dent   ac ci den tal   15. maj es ty   ma jes tic
8. ir ri gate   ir ri ga tion   16. e lec tric   e lec tric i ty

Complete each sentence below with a word from the word box.

WORD BOX

| microscopic | electricity | irrigation | alphabetical |
| original | librarian | historical | mysterious |

1. The _____ showed Max where the books about football were kept.

2. I arranged my DVDs in _____ order by title.

3. Many important events happened in the _____ city of Philadelphia.

4. The storm knocked out the _____ and left many homes with no heat.

5. Is this the _____ painting or a copy of it?

6. The dry desert was changed into rich, green farmland by _____.

7. These _____ germs are so small that you can't see them.

Sometimes a shift in accent changes the meaning of the word.

re•fuse[1] /rē fūz´/, **1.** to say no to something: *He refused to wear his boots.* **2.** to say one is not willing to do or give something: *They refused to accept the money. verb,* **re•fused, re•fus•ing.**

ref•use[2] /ref´ yūs/, useless material; waste. *noun.*

Pronounce the pairs of words in the word box. Then complete each sentence below with one of the words. Include its accent mark.

──────────────── **WORD BOX** ────────────────

pro duce´	pro test´	in crease´	con tent´
pro´ duce	pro´ test	in´ crease	con´ tent
sus pect´	per fect´	re cord´	ob ject´
sus´ pect	per´ fect	rec´ ord	ob´ ject

1. Dad does not _____ to the loud TV, but Mom does.

2. The _____ marchers carried signs in front of City Hall.

3. It takes many workers to _____ a new car.

4. On my birthday, I got an _____ in my allowance.

5. Doctors _____ that a virus causes the disease.

6. The inventor worked to _____ the machine.

7. The _____ of the car wash is to raise money for the band.

8. I play several bingo cards at once to _____ my chances of winning.

9. It did the player no good to _____ the umpire's call.

10. The _____ of some popular foods is not healthy.

11. I think it's fun to _____ a message on my phone.

12. The police officer chased the _____ down the alley.

13. Not many people score a _____ 300 in bowling.

14. The _____ stand was full of fresh fruit and vegetables.

Pronunciation Key

a	cat	ā	cake	ä	father	ch	chin	e	red	ē	see	ėr her
g	get	i	big	ī	ride	j	jump	ng	ring	o	stop	ō hope
ô	talk	oi	noise	ou	out	s	sit	sh	shall	th	thank	
th	then	u	cut	u̇	put	ü	rule	yū	cute	zh	pleasure	
ə about, spoken, giraffe, police, picture								z	rose			

Underline the respelling of the word that correctly completes each sentence.

1. Rosa used a (tak, tāk, tuk) to hang her drawing on the wall.

2. Corn, wheat, and rice are different kinds of (grēn, grān, grin).

3. It's dangerous to pull a (kär, sher, cher) out from under someone.

4. My older brother does not like to (lēnd, land, lend) me his bike.

5. What's the difference between a (fėrm, färm, fôrm) and a ranch?

6. Andy wears (sēz, sez, sīz) seven shoes.

7. My family gave me a new (rub, rob, rōb) when I was in the hospital.

8. Ban Mo (thôt, tôt, thō) we were leaving at nine o'clock.

9. The cold potatoes sat in a (lam, lump, lamp) on Colleen's plate.

10. It's a (sām, chum, shām) Dad didn't see your skateboard before moving the car.

11. Ramón likes to (wāk, wôk, wėrk) through the park on warm spring days.

12. We need three more points to (wun, wīn, win) the championship.

Write the respelling of each word below.

1. did _____

2. hat _____

3. step _____

4. train _____

5. five _____

6. eat _____

7. not _____

8. duck _____

9. show _____

10. ice _____

Pronunciation Key

a cat	ā cake	ä father	ch chin	e red	ē see	ėr her
g get	i big	ī ride	j jump	ng ring	o stop	ō hope
ô talk	oi noise	ou out	s sit	sh shall		th thank
th then	u cut	u̇ put	ü rule	yū cute		zh pleasure
ə about, spoken, giraffe, police, picture				z rose		

Complete each sentence with one of the respellings below it.

1. The northern _____ of the island was a wide, sandy beach.

                        kōst   gōst   chōz

2. Does this box _____ fossils or rocks?

                        kən fyüz´   kən fes´   kən tān´

3. The brothers often _____ over who will mow the lawn.

                        ə rōz´   är´ gyü   ə rest´

4. I can't understand what you say when you _____.

                        mum´ bəl   mus´ əl   mam´ əl

5. Do you _____ any of the new television shows?

                        en´ jən   en joi´   in vent´

6. The cook added bananas to the delicious _____.

                        pud´ l   pu̇d´ ing   pyü´ pəl

In front of each respelling below, write the letter of its definition.

____ 1. mezh´ ər   a. a light rainfall

____ 2. shal´ ō   b. a person who lives in a small town

____ 3. shou´ ər   c. to cover up with earth

____ 4. bėr´ ō   d. not deep

____ 5. ber´ ē   e. a sour liquid

____ 6. vin´ ə gər   f. a hole dug in the ground by an animal

____ 7. vil´ i jər   g. to find the size of something

Many words have more than one meaning. In the dictionary, each separate meaning is numbered.

Read these dictionary entries for **bridge** and **hand**. Then read the sentences below. On the line, write the number of the definition that matches the use of the word in the sentence.

bridge /brij/, **1.** a structure built over a road, river, or railroad: *The new bridge was opened to traffic yesterday.* **2.** an area above the deck of a ship for the commanding officer: *The captain watched the approaching storm from the bridge.* **3.** the upper bony part of the nose: *Her glasses kept sliding down over the bridge of her nose.* **4.** a mounting which holds false teeth attached to real teeth: *Gram's new bridge is not ready yet.* **5.** the movable piece over which the strings of a violin, cello, etc., are stretched: *The bridge of my violin broke just before my solo.* **6.** to make a way over something: *A log bridged the stream.* 1–5 *noun*, 6. *verb*, **bridged, bridg•ing.**

hand /hand/, **1.** the end part of the arm with four fingers and a thumb: *That glove is too big for my hand.* **2.** something that is like a hand: *the hands on a clock.* **3.** a paid worker: *a farm hand.* **4.** possession; control: *The matter is out of my hands.* **5.** a share in doing something: *I didn't have a hand in arranging the party.* **6.** side: *To my right hand is Mrs. Wang.* **7.** a handwriting style: *His letters are always in a dark, heavy hand.* **8.** skill: *He tried his hand at painting.* **9.** a promise to marry: *The prince asked for her hand.* **10.** the width of a hand; 4 inches: *A Shetland pony is about 9 hands high.* **11.** to give or pass with the hand: *Please hand me the salt.* **12.** to help with the hand: *The nurse handed the patient into a bed.* 1–10 *noun*, 11–12 *verb*.

For *bridge:*

_____ **1.** A thick board was used to bridge the gap between the rocks.

_____ **2.** The ball cracked my nose right at the bridge.

_____ **3.** The old covered bridge across that creek is falling down.

_____ **4.** The dentist fitted Granddad with a new bridge.

_____ **5.** After giving the signal to dive, the captain ran from the submarine bridge.

For *hand:*

_____ **6.** During summer vacation, Paul worked as a farm hand.

_____ **7.** "Happy Birthday" was written in a neat hand across the card.

_____ **8.** When playing gets out of hand, someone often gets hurt.

_____ **9.** The hands on Ricardo's watch glow in the dark.

_____ **10.** Kayla cannot throw a ball well with her left hand.

Homographs are words that are spelled alike but have different meanings. Sometimes they are pronounced differently, too. In a dictionary, homographs are listed as separate entry words with a small number placed after each one.

On the line in front of each sentence, write the number of the homograph used in that sentence. Do not write the number of the definition.

bark¹ /bärk/, **1.** the outside covering of the trunk, branches, and roots of trees. **2.** to rub or scrape the skin off. 1 *noun,* 2 *verb.*

bark² /bärk/, **1.** the short, loud noise made by a dog. **2.** to shout or speak loudly or gruffly. 1 *noun,* 2 *verb.*

_____ **1.** All of the puppies in the pet shop began to bark at the same time.

_____ **2.** The woodpecker tapped quickly through the bark to find its lunch.

_____ **3.** Brian barked his knee when he fell on the sidewalk.

_____ **4.** The coach barked loudly at the lazy members of the team.

file¹ /fīl/, **1.** a folder, drawer, case, etc., for keeping papers and records in order. **2.** the papers or records kept in order. **3.** an orderly row of persons or things. **4.** to put in order. **5.** to march or move in an orderly way. 1–3 *noun,* 4–5 *verb,* **filed, fil•ing.**

file² /fīl/, **1.** a steel tool with many small, sharp ridges or teeth to smooth or wear away hard materials. **2.** to smoooth or wear away with a file. 1 *noun,* 2 *verb,* **filed, fil•ing.**

_____ **5.** Mom keeps our family records in a file on the computer.

_____ **6.** Stand in single file to wait for the bus.

_____ **7.** It's better to file your fingernails than to cut them.

_____ **8.** The plumber used a file to smooth the end of the copper pipe.

tear¹ /tir/, drop of salty liquid that keeps the eyeball moist. *noun.*

tear² /tēr or tãr/, **1.** to pull apart by force. **2.** to make by ripping or pulling apart. **3.** to cut deeply. **4.** to divide or split by opposite forces. **5.** to remove by force. **6.** to move with great haste. **7.** a torn place. 1–6 *verb,* **tore, torn, tear•ing;** 7 *noun.*

_____ **9.** A huge crane will be used to tear down the old post office.

_____ **10.** It will be easier to tear that paper if you fold it first.

_____ **11.** A single tear rolled down the man's cheek.

_____ **12.** When the saw began to tear into the thick tree trunk, wood chips went flying.

Homophones are words that sound alike but are spelled differently and have different meanings.

pare /pēr or pār/, **1.** to cut or shave off the outside part of something; to peel. **2.** to make smaller little by little. *verb.*

pear /pēr or pār/, **1.** a sweet fruit larger and more rounded at one end and smaller at the stem end. **2.** the tree on which this fruit grows. *noun.*

On each line, write a homophone for the word given.

1. oh _____

2. vein _____

3. peek _____

4. tied _____

5. heel _____

6. waste _____

7. board _____

8. pane _____

9. piece _____

10. mail _____

Read the paragraph below. On each line write one of the homophones given below it.

I have a new _____ of friends. Carlos and Isabel arrived
pair, pear

_____ last _____ from Puerto Rico. They
here, hear   weak, week

made the trip by _____. Each of them _____ how to
plain, plane   knows, nose

_____ and _____ in both English and Spanish.
read, reed   right, write

Carlos and Isabel say that in Puerto Rico, the weather is almost always

_____. They have never even _____ snow.
fair, fare   scene, seen

Puerto Rico has beautiful beaches, mountains, and a _____
rain, rein

forest. Yet the _____ island is _____ even as
hole, whole   knot, not

large as the state of Connecticut.

Synonyms are words that have the same, or almost the same, meaning.

Read the paragraphs below. In them, find a synonym for each numbered word. Write it on the line after the word.

The game is about to begin. People fill the stands. The weather is mild, and the sky is beautiful. The large crowd shouts. Everyone watches as the players dash onto the field from a dark tunnel.

Does this sound like a football game on a fall afternoon? It could be. Or it could have happened in ancient Greece. In Greece, scientists have found the remains of a stadium more than 2,000 years old. They have learned that the stadiums of today and those of long ago are quite alike. However, some of the games are different. There were races and championship fights. One event was called the hammer throw. Another contest was held to see who could throw a spear farthest. The Greek people went to see their games just as today's fans do.

It was the stadium tunnel that most excited the scientists, though. On its stone walls, the Greek sports heroes had carved their names. The results of the events were recorded, too. So there's one thing that the scientists know for sure. Sports fans and players have not changed much during all these years.

1. game _____

2. start _____

3. big _____

4. view _____

5. similar _____

6. pretty _____

7. toss _____

8. rock _____

9. discovered _____

10. certain _____

11. looks _____

12. rush _____

13. yells _____

14. written _____

15. old _____

16. autumn _____

Read the paragraphs below. In them, find an antonym for each numbered word. Write it on the line after the word.

Have you read the book *Around the World in Eighty Days?* In it, a man named Phileas Fogg travels around the world in a hot air balloon. Many people who first read the story in 1873 thought it was true. However, it was just a good story.

That same year, 1873, marked the first time someone crossed the Atlantic Ocean in a balloon. Strong winds and bad weather ended that trip. Other people also tried, but the weather always won. Some of these travelers were lucky enough to get rescued from the cold water. Others died.

Finally, in 1978, three Americans succeeded in making the difficult journey. That was 105 years after the first try! The name of their large balloon was the Double Eagle II. It was 120 feet high. The top half was silver, and the rest was black. The men took off from the United States on a Friday. They came down almost six days later in France. Many people came to greet them. The good news flashed around the world.

1. before _____

2. up _____

3. hot _____

4. bad _____

5. last _____

6. small _____

7. began _____

8. bottom _____

9. false _____

10. lost _____

11. lived _____

12. failed _____

13. low _____

14. easy _____

15. few _____

16. weak _____

chap¹ /chap/, **1.** to crack or open in slits: *My hands were chapped from the cold air.* **2.** to make rough: *The cold weather chapped his face.* verb, **chapped, chap•ping.**

chap² /chap/, a fellow; a man or boy. *noun.*

chart /chärt/, **1.** a map, especially one that shows the coasts, rocks, reefs, currents, and depths of a sea. **2.** a sheet of information given in pictures, tables, lists, or diagrams. **3.** to make a chart: *The teacher charted the reading progress of each student.* 1–2 *noun,* 3 *verb.*

chick /chik/, **1.** a young bird, especially a young chicken. **2.** a child. *noun.*

chim•pan•zee /chim pan´ zē´ or chim pan´ zē/, an intelligent African ape, not as large as a gorilla. *noun.*

chirp /chėrp/, **1.** the short, quick sound made by some insects and small birds: *the chirp of a cricket.* **2.** to make this short, quick sound. 1 *noun,* 2 *verb.*

chunk /chungk/, a short, thick piece or lump of something: *He cut the cheese into chunks. noun.*

churn /chėrn/, **1.** a container in which butter is made from milk or cream by beating, stirring, or shaking. **2.** to beat, stir, or shake in a churn. **3.** to move as if being beaten, stirred, or shaken: *My stomach was churning with hunger.* 1 *noun,* 2–3 *verb.*

cin•der /sin´ dər/, **1.** a piece of partly burned wood or coal that may continue to burn but will no longer flame. **2.** completely burned wood or coal; ash. *noun.*

cit•y /sit´ ē/, **1.** a large, important town, usually one that manages its own affairs: *Which city do you live closest to—San Francisco, Chicago, or Pittsburgh?* **2.** the people who live in a city: *As the city slept, it snowed and snowed.* **3.** of or in a city: *The city schools will open next week.* 1–2 *noun,* plural **cit•ies;** 3 *adjective.*

clum•sy /klum´ zē/. **1.** not having skill or grace in moving; awkward: *The clumsy puppy tripped over the carpet.* **2.** not well made, well done, or well shaped: *The clumsy bookshelf could hold only a few books.* adjective, **clum•si•er, clum•si•est.**

---

1. What are the guide words on this page? _____

2. Circle the words that would come before this page.   chant   check   change

3. Circle the words that would come after this page.   clue   clutch   clung

4. How many entry words are shown? _____

5. Which spelling has two entries? _____

6. Which entry word has three syllables? _____

7. Which entry word has two pronunciations? _____

8. Under which entry word does **clumsier** appear? _____

9. Which entry words have the same vowel sound as **her?** _____

In each row, underline the synonym and circle the antonym of the first word.

1. **bold**	hot	cowardly	brave	few
2. **defend**	guard	lean	against	attack
3. **future**	past	hereafter	last	alone
4. **mend**	groan	crowd	destroy	repair
5. **ordinary**	usual	stop	rare	catch
6. **sadness**	fairness	sorrow	dryness	glee
7. **rough**	smooth	uneven	boat	fall
8. **remain**	forget	between	stay	depart
9. **seldom**	rarely	quiet	top	often
10. **personal**	none	public	private	young

In the first column below, write the homophone from the word box. In the second column, write the homograph for which two meanings are given.

WORD BOX

hose	people	noon	pear	brake
hail	pane	pupil	store	date
knot	note	heel	punch	mist
firm	juice	pure	mail	meal

1. pain _____

2. male _____

3. break _____

4. hoes _____

5. heal _____

6. not _____

7. missed _____

8. pare _____

9. solid _____

   a business

10. a student _____

   the black of an eye

11. to hit _____

   a sweet drink

12. a certain time _____

   a palm tree fruit

Circle the word with the same vowel sound as the first word in the row.

1. **shoe**   show   group   shop   poet

2. **dry**   dairy   cape   kit   slide

3. **rope**   top   bowl   do   soon

4. **team**   break   tame   green   tram

5. **lunch**   soup   quilt   guest   drum

6. **crate**   track   eight   grab   coat

7. **bread**   dream   squeeze   fresh   new

8. **coin**   rain   joy   chin   crime

9. **house**   soup   show   crown   loose

10. **huge**   mule   blue   school   urge

Write the word for each pronunciation.

1. /bā′ kə rē/ _____

2. /en′ tər tān′/ _____

3. /lō′ kəl/ _____

4. /ōv′ ər nīt′/ _____

5. /skī′ rok it/ _____

6. /sak′ sə fōn′/ _____

7. /jen′ təl mən/ _____

8. /op′ ər tū′ ni tē/ _____

9. /pē′ pəl/ _____

10. /miks′ chur/ _____

11. /fīr′ plās′/ _____

12. /kôl/ _____

13. /dān′ jər əs/ _____

14. /nach′ ər əl/ _____

15. /kon′ sen trā′ shən/ _____

Write the plural form of each word.

1. watch _____   6. hero _____

2. calf _____   7. bunny _____

3. toe _____   8. five _____

4. holiday _____   9. box _____

5. chair _____   10. trophy _____

Write each phrase as a possessive phrase.

1. the claws of the cat _____

2. the tails of the dogs _____

3. the feathers of the robin _____

4. the whiskers of the mice _____

5. the leaves of the bushes _____

Rewrite each sentence using plural and possessive forms of the nouns.

The face of Ruth and Jenny were visible through the window of the garage.

_____

_____

The brake of the truck squealed, and the owner held the leash of the dog.

_____

_____

Change the meaning of each word by adding a prefix.

_____happy   _____spell   _____possible

_____agree   _____complete   _____fiction

Add a suffix to each word. Write the new word in the sentence.

direct   1. You're going in the wrong _____.

argue   2. The two drivers had an _____ after the accident.

happy   3. You can see the _____ in Kevin's eyes.

invite   4. We received an _____ to the wedding.

visit   5. Franz is the five-hundredth _____ to the museum.

ambition   6. The students have taken on an _____ project.

nature   7. It is _____ to want to win.

change   8. Eileen has a _____ personality.

care   9. You should not be _____ when you cross the street.

moss   10. Do not slip on the _____ rocks.

pharmacy   11. The _____ will fill your prescription.

beauty   12. The moon is _____ tonight.

child   13. My younger brother is very _____.

protect   14. Take a flashlight for your own _____.

Write the base word of each word.

1. unimaginable _____   4. prehistoric _____

2. misjudgment _____   5. reproducible _____

3. inactivity _____   6. dishonesty _____

four /fôr/ one more than three and one less than five. *noun.*

fox /foks/ a wild animal that resembles a small dog. A fox has pointed ears, a long nose, and a bushy tail. *noun,* plural: **foxes.**

freedom /frē´ dəm/ **1.** the state of being free: *Our forefathers fought to gain freedom for us.* **2.** being able to move about without being held back: *On the farm we have the freedom to do as we please. noun.*

freeway /frē´ wā´/ a highway with several lanes and no stoplights. *noun.*

freeze /frēz/ **1.** to turn to ice because of cold temperatures. *Water can freeze outdoors in winter.* **2.** to become very cold. *verb.* **froze, freezing, frozen.**

French /french/ **1.** the language spoken by people in France. **2.** with *the,* people who live in France: *The French make good cheese.* **3.** about people or things in France. 1-2 *noun,* 3 *adjective.*

frenzy /fren´ zē/ a state of great excitement. *The dog was in a frenzy because the cat jumped on its back. noun.*

frequent /frē´ kwent/ often; happening many times. *Mom has frequent meetings at night. adjective;* **frequently,** *adverb.*

friend /frend/ a person one likes. *I had lunch with a good friend. noun,* plural: **friends.**

friendly /frend´ lē/ acting like a friend. *We gave each other a friendly wave. adjective.* **friendlier, friendliest.**

1. What are the guide words on this page? _____

2. Which entry word begins with a capital letter? _____

3. Which entry word is related to the word before it? _____

4. Which three entry words have the same first syllable? _____

5. Which entry word is a verb? _____

6. Circle the entry word that would come before this page.

          fountain   freckle   frighten

7. Circle the entry word that would come after this page.

      French fries   frontier   framework

8. Which entry word is a compound word? _____

9. How many entry words have just one syllable? _____

10. Which entry word can be two parts of speech? _____